7 STEPS TO GROWING RICH

YOUR MOST
VALUABLE
ASSET

BRIAN TRACY

New York Times Bestselling Author

simple ▶ truths
small books: **BIG IMPACT.**

Photo Credits
Cover: front, Mliberra/Shutterstock, hchjjl/Shutterstock
Internals: page 1, Mliberra/Shutterstock, hchjjl/Shutterstock; pages 2–3, ma_rish/
Shutterstock; page 7, hugolacasse/iStock; pages 10–11, OnBlast/iStock, Paul Lesser/
Shutterstock; page 17, DvdArts/iStock; page 24, aleksandarvelasevic/iStock

Published by Simple Truths, an imprint of Sourcebooks, Inc.
P.O. Box 4410, Naperville, Illinois 60567–4410
(630) 961-3900
Fax: (630) 961-2168
www.sourcebooks.com

Printed and bound in China.
QL 10 9 8 7 6 5 4 3 2 1

CONTENTS

INTRODUCTION

Your most valuable financial asset is your ability to earn money. This can be defined as your ability to get results that people will pay you for. Unless you are already rich, your earning ability, or *earning power*, represents 80 to 90 percent of your financial value.

Properly applied to the marketplace, your earning ability is a *well*. By maximizing your earning ability and getting results that people will pay you for, you can pump tens of thousands of dollars a year into your pocket.

All your knowledge, education, skills, and experience in life have contributed to the person you are today and to your ability to get results for which someone will pay good money.

Your earning ability is like farmland—if you don't take excellent care of it by cultivating and tending to it on a regular basis—it soon loses its ability to produce the kind of harvest you desire. Successful men and women are those who are extremely aware of the importance and value of their earning abilities. They treat it as a valuable and precious asset. They work every day to keep increasing its productive value—in order to keep it current with the demands of the marketplace.

An Appreciating Asset

Your earning ability, like any asset, can *appreciate* or *depreciate*. It can regularly increase in value, enabling you to earn more and more with each passing year. Or it can depreciate, losing value as the markets change and your skills become less and less in demand.

Here is the hard truth: if you are not becoming more and more valuable by continuously and aggressively upgrading your skills, you are *automatically* falling behind, as the market itself is always changing and moving. If your earning ability is not appreciating, it is *automatically* depreciating.

There are millions of unemployed and underemployed people today who have let their earning ability decline so far that no one will hire them to get the few results they are still capable of generating. And most of them do not even know what has happened.

Make a Decision

What is the key to increasing your income? Make a decision! From this day forward, decide that you are going to earn the amount of money you are truly capable of earning. Make a decision that you will take complete control of your career and your income so you can survive and thrive in any economy.

Decide today that you are going to *double your income* and then double it again. Make a decision that you are going to earn more and more until you fulfill your true potential as an earning machine.

Learn What You Need to Learn

In the pages ahead, you will learn a series of practical, proven strategies, methods, and techniques that you can use immediately to begin earning what you are really worth. The best news is that the amount you are truly worth is vastly *greater* than anything you have ever enjoyed up to now.

Remember, it doesn't matter where you're coming *from;* all that really matters is where you're *going*. And where you're going is limited only by your imagination.

Your very highest income, best accomplishments, proudest achievements, and happiest moments lie in the future. The greatest successes of your life are still to come. This book will show you how to reach them.

It's Your Decision

You are earning today exactly the amount you have decided to earn, no more and no less. You are where you are financially because you have chosen to be there. Only you. No one else.

You have decided to earn this amount as a result of your *actions* as well as your *inactions*. There are specific actions you have taken to get your income to the point where it is today. And there are actions that you have failed to take that have caused your income to stay far below what you are truly capable of earning. But whatever you are earning today, you have decided to earn that amount.

You Are Free to Choose

When I first heard the idea that I was determining my own income, I was shocked and angry. I denied it vigorously. "That's not true," I said. "No one would choose to earn *this* small amount of money, and then worry about money all the time!"

I blamed my low income on my parents, my education, my boss, my company, my industry, the competition, and the economy. Then I looked around me, and realized that there were hundreds and even thousands of people who had the same problems and limitations I did but who were earning far more than I was and living much better lives.

I finally accepted that I was where I was and what I was because of *me*. If I was not happy about my life and my income, there was only one person in the world who could change it—me. This awakening changed my life.

Five years later, I had increased my income ten times over! I went from living in a rented apartment with rented furniture to driving my own dream car, a Mercedes-Benz 450SEL, parking it in my spacious double garage attached to my dream home in an expensive neighborhood. My whole life was transformed, and yours can be as well.

CHAPTER ONE

UNLOCK YOUR EARNING POTENTIAL

$\longrightarrow$

*"I am always doing that which I cannot do,
in order that I may learn how to do it."*

–Pablo Picasso

THROUGHOUT MOST OF HUMAN HISTORY, we have become accustomed to *evolution*, or the gradual progression of events in a straight line. Sometimes the process of change has been faster, and sometimes it has been slower, but it has almost always seemed to move steadily forward, allowing sufficient time for planning, predicting, and changing.

Today, however, the rate of change is not only faster than ever before, but it is *discontinuous*. It takes place in a variety of unconnected areas and affects each of us in a multitude of unexpected ways. Changes in information technology are happening separately from changes in medicine, transportation, education, politics, or global competition.

Changes in family formation and relationships are happening separately from the rise and fall of new businesses and industries in different parts of the country and the world. And if anything, this rate of accelerated, discontinuous change is *increasing*. As a result, most of us are already suffering from what author Alvin Toffler once called *future shock*.

Your choice of a career, and a job within that career, is one of the most important decisions you ever make. Unfortunately, most people drift into their jobs, accepting whatever is offered to them at the time and then allowing other people to determine what they will do, where and how they will do it, and how much they will be paid for it.

The company and the boss become much like an extension of the mother and the father, taking care of everything. This creates a natural inertia, a resistance to any change in direction or speed. This inertia carries most people onward through their careers, month after month and year after year.

The Market Is Tough and Getting Tougher

The marketplace is a stern taskmaster. Today, excellence, quality, and value are absolutely essential elements of any product or service and of the work of any person. Your earning ability is largely determined by the perception of excellence, quality, and value that others have of you and what you do.

The market only pays excellent rewards for *excellent* performance. It pays average rewards for average performance, and it pays below-average rewards (or unemployment) for below-average performance.

Customers want the very most, and the very best, on the very best terms, for the very least amount of money. Only those individuals and companies that provide absolutely excellent products and services at absolutely excellent prices will survive. It's not personal; it's just the way our economy works.

To *earn* more, you must *learn* more. You are maxed out today at your current level of knowledge and skill. What you are earning at this moment is the maximum you can earn without learning and practicing something new and different.

Continuous Learning

The solution to the dilemma of unavoidable change and restructuring is continuous *self-improvement*. Your personal knowledge and your ability to apply it are your most valuable assets. To stay on top, you must continually add to your knowledge and skills—repeatedly building up your mental assets if you want to enjoy a consistently high return on your investment. It is only by building on your current assets that you can stop them from deteriorating.

By engaging in continuous self-improvement, you put yourself behind the wheel of your own life. Dedicating yourself to increasing your earning ability will engage you in the never-ending process of personal and professional development. By learning more, you prepare yourself to earn more. You position yourself for tomorrow by developing the knowledge and skills that you need to be a valuable and productive part of our economy, no matter which direction it goes.

Your Knowledge and Skills Are Investments

Here's a key point: your education, knowledge, skills, and experience are all investments in your ability to contribute a value for which you can be paid. But they are like any other investments. They are highly speculative.

Once you have learned a subject or developed a skill, it is time and money spent that you cannot get back. No employer in the marketplace has any obligation to pay you for your past skill and experience, unless he or she can use your skill to produce a product or service that people are ready to buy *today*.

Whatever job you are doing, you should be preparing for your *next* job. The key questions are always:

➡ Where are the customers?
➡ What do people want to buy?
➡ Which businesses and industries are serving customers the best?

➡ Which businesses are growing in this economy, and
which are declining?

When people who ask me how they can increase their income
when their entire industry is shrinking, I tell them that there are
jobs with futures and jobs *without* futures, and they need to get
into a field that is expanding, not contracting.

There Are Always Lots of Jobs

There are three forms of unemployment: *voluntary*, *involuntary*, and
frictional. Voluntary unemployment is when a person decides not to
work for a certain period of time, or not to accept a particular type
of job, hoping that something better will come along. Involuntary
unemployment occurs when a person is willing and able to work
but cannot find a job anywhere. Frictional unemployment is the
natural level, which includes the approximately 4 or 5 percent of
the working population who are between jobs at any given time.

However, there are always jobs for the creative minority. You never have to be unemployed if you will do one of three things: First, you can change the work that you are offering to do. Second, you can change the place where you are offering to work. And third, you can change the amount that you are asking for your services.

If there is no demand for your particular skills and experience, you will have to learn to do something else and provide skills that are in demand right now. Employers don't care about your past. They care only about your future and your ability to contribute value to their customers.

You can also change your *location*. Sometimes you will have to move from one part of the country to another, from where there are few jobs to where there are more. Many people transform their entire lives by moving from an area of high unemployment to an area of low unemployment. In job seeking, you must "fish where the fish are."

Be Prepared to Work for Less

The third thing you can do to get back into the workforce is to lower your demands. Remember, because your labor is a *commodity*, it is subject to the laws of supply and demand. If you ask for too much, people will not hire you, because customers will not pay your demands through the price of the product or service that your organization produces. It is not the employer who is forcing this downward revision in wages; it is the customer, through his or her buying behavior.

There is a small, creative minority who are *never* unemployed. No matter what happens, they always have a job—sometimes two jobs. If they lose a particular position in one place, they find another position doing the same thing, or something else, somewhere else. They are fast on their feet. They move quickly, and they don't accept unemployment as an option. They always have jobs. This must be your strategy as well.

Even in the worst economy, there are always problems to be solved and consumer needs to be met. For this reason, all long-term unemployment is ultimately *voluntary*. People are consciously or unconsciously choosing not to participate in the workforce.

There are as many opportunities for you to fulfill your dreams and aspirations in the U.S. economy today as there have ever been. There are thousands of jobs advertised online every day—and even more that aren't advertised. You can be, have, or do anything that you can dream of by preparing yourself for better and better jobs. It is never crowded at the top. As Zig Ziglar said, "There are no traffic jams on the extra mile." Your goal must be to get good, get even better, and then make yourself indispensable.

Double Your Income?

Would you like to double your income? When I ask this in my seminars, everyone usually raises their hand, nods, and shouts out, "Yes!"

I then go on to tell them that they are in luck. As an economist, I can assure them that everyone in the room is going to double his or her income—*if they live long enough.*

"The average income goes up at about 3 percent per annum," I explain. "Therefore, if you live and work for another twenty-two years, increasing your income at 3 percent per annum, with compound interest, you will double your income. Is that what you had in mind?"

Everyone then replies, "No!" Everyone wants to double his or her income much sooner than in twenty-two years. The good news is that there are people all around you who are increasing their income at far more rapid rates than 3 percent per year, and your goal should be to be one of them.

Increase Your Contribution

Economic basics say that you must contribute three to six dollars of profit, or even more, for every dollar that you wish to earn in salary. In terms of space, benefits, training, supervision, and investment in furniture, fixtures, and other resources, it costs a company a minimum of twice your basic salary to employ you.

For a company to hire you, they have to make a *profit* on what they pay you. Therefore, you must contribute value greatly in excess of the amount you earn in order to stay employed. To put it another way, your contribution must be considerably greater than the amount you are receiving, or you will find yourself looking for another job.

The Future Belongs to the Competent

To position yourself for tomorrow, here is one of the most important rules you will ever learn: *The future belongs to the competent*. The future belongs to those men and women who are good at what they do and are getting better. As Pat Riley wrote in his book *The Winner Within*, "If you are not committed to getting better at what you are doing, you are bound to get worse." To phrase it another way, anything less than a commitment to excellent performance on your part is an unconscious acceptance of mediocrity.

It used to be that you needed to be excellent to rise above the competition in your industry. Today, you must be excellent even to keep your job for the long term.

Use Compound Interest in Your Favor

If your income increases by 11 percent per annum, you will double your income in six and a half years. And in six and a half years more, you'll double it again. You can do this again and again. Soon, you will be living in a lovely house in a beautiful neighborhood, driving an expensive car, and sending your kids to private schools. Because of the law of compound interest, if your income keeps increasing, every element of your financial and personal life will improve at the same rate.

I have worked with salespeople and business owners who learned what you are going to learn in this book, and they went from earning less than $20,000 per year to more than $1,000,000 a year in income in less than ten years. Compound interest and compound growth can be your best friends.

CHAPTER TWO

TAKE CHARGE OF YOUR INCOME

"You must take personal responsibility. You cannot change the circumstances, the seasons, or the wind, but you can change yourself. That is something you have charge of."

–Jim Rohn

AN ATTITUDE OF SELF-RESPONSIBILITY GOES hand in hand with success, happiness, self-control, and high earnings in every area of life. Researchers have discovered that the top 3 percent of workers in every field had a special attitude that made them stand out. They saw themselves as *self-employed*. They acted as if they personally owned the companies they worked for. They accepted responsibility for everything that happened to their companies—as well as for results. When you develop this attitude, you immediately move onto the fast track in your career.

The biggest mistake you can make is to ever think that you work for anyone other than *yourself*. No matter who signs your paycheck, you are always self-employed, from the time you take your first job until the day you retire. You are the head of an entrepreneurial enterprise with one employee—yourself—responsible for selling one product—your personal services.

Put another way, you are the *president* of your own personal service corporation and the chief executive officer of your own life. You are completely responsible for the business of your life and for everything that happens to both it and you. You are in charge of production, marketing, quality control, finance, and research and development.

You Write Your Own Paycheck

You ultimately determine your own salary and write your own paycheck. If you are not happy with the amount that you are earning, go to the nearest mirror and negotiate with your boss. We are each where we are and what we are because that is where and what we have decided to be. If you are not happy with any part of your career, it is up to you to make whatever changes are necessary to bring about a better state of affairs.

When you are the president of your own personal service corporation, everything that affects the business you work for affects your personal business as well. You no longer have the luxury of standing aside and looking at the rate of change, thinking that it affects other people but not you. Losers say, "That's not my job." Winners say, "This is my company; *everything* is my job."

Every innovation, discovery, and paradigm shift in modern business is as applicable to you as it is to a multibillion-dollar corporation. Every piece of information generated by management and business thinkers that can affect your business in some way relates to you.

The men and women who will survive and thrive in the years ahead are those who continually look for ideas and insights that they can use to be faster, more flexible, and more effective in their work on a day-to-day basis.

As is the case for the presidents of all high-achieving companies, your goal is to be a *market leader*. In fact, if you are not committed to being the best in your field, you are not getting better—and you are probably getting *worse*. If you are not committed to being one of the top 10 percent of the people in your field, you will end up somewhere far below.

The Seven Rs of Personal Management

To maximize your potential for career success, you should engage in the seven Rs of modern management:

Rethinking, Reevaluating, Reorganizing, Restructuring, Reengineering, Reinventing, and Refocusing.

1. Rethink Your Situation

In *rethinking*, you take time on a regular basis to think about who you are and where you are going, especially when you feel discontented or dissatisfied for any reason. Since everything is changing so rapidly around you, more options are available to you now than ever before. And because it is very likely that you are going to be doing something completely different in a few years anyway, you can begin thinking today about where you want to be in the future. You can rethink and replan your entire career.

2. Reevaluate Your Situation

Reevaluating is the process of standing back and looking at yourself in terms of the marketplace. Whenever you experience stress, frustration, or roadblocks in your work or career, you need to take time to reevaluate your situation and make sure that you are on the right track.

Your problems may be caused by your working at the wrong job, at the wrong company, or with the wrong people. Your dissatisfaction may be caused by selling a product or service that is wrong for you, or for many other reasons.

Perhaps your heart is no longer in your work. It gives you little or no pleasure. Sometimes, the very best thing to do in a situation like this is to change the work you are doing or the company for which you are working, so that your work life is more consistent with your talents, abilities, desires, and values.

3. Reorganize Your Life

In *reorganization*, you examine your daily activities and question whether or not you should be doing things differently if you want  to get better results. Look for ways to work with greater efficiency and perform your tasks faster and better. Always try to increase your output relative to your input of time and money.

4. Restructure Your Activities

In *restructuring*, look at the specific things you do that contribute the most value to your company and to your customers. Focus more and more of your time and talent on the 20 percent of your activities that contribute 80 percent of the value.

Concentrate on those activities that represent the highest payoff for everyone involved.

5. Reengineer Your Career

In *reengineering* your personal services corporation, stand back and look at the entire process of your work, from the first thing you do in the morning to the actual results that you get for your company or your customer.

Analyze this process and look for ways to streamline your work by reducing steps, consolidating activities, outsourcing parts of the work, and even changing the process completely so that you can achieve the same or better results with less time and fewer resources. Reengineering is an ongoing process of *simplifying* your work and your activities so you can get more done in less time.

6. Reinvent Yourself Regularly

In *reinventing*, you stand back from your work and imagine starting over again. Imagine that your job or industry disappeared completely. Imagine for a moment that you had to move across the street or across the country and begin your career or your business all over.

What would you do differently? Where would you want to be in three to five years? What changes would you have to make to create the future that you desire?

One of the best ways to reinvent yourself is to determine what it is that you really enjoy doing more than anything else, and then to begin figuring out how you can find or create a job doing more of it.

7. Refocus Your Energies

The final R stands for *refocusing*. This is really the key to the future.

It is your ability to concentrate your energies single-mindedly on doing those few things that make all the difference in your life.

In most cases, people are unsuccessful because they spend too much time doing things that contribute little to their lives. They spend more and more time doing things that have less and less value. On the other hand, highly successful people do a small number of tasks, but the few things they do, they do extremely well. This seems to be the secret to great success and achievement in every area of life.

Become a Master of Change

The advantage of practicing the seven Rs, of focusing on the disciplines that enable you to be a leader in your field and master the forces of change, is that they allow you to *regain control* over your present and future. With a sense of control comes a feeling of personal power and greater self-confidence. When you design your own life and future, rather than allowing them to be determined by the unpredictable winds of change, you feel happier, healthier, and more powerful in everything you do.

You are responsible. Think of yourself as the president of your own personal service corporation. See yourself as being in charge of your own life. When you begin to see yourself as an active participant in the dynamic world around you, you take full control of your own destiny. You become the architect of your own future and the primary creative force in your own life.

An ATTITUDE of self-responsibility goes hand in hand with success, happiness, self-control, and high earnings in every area of LIFE.

CHAPTER THREE

DO WHAT YOU DO BEST

"One's only security in life comes from doing something uncommonly well."

—Abraham Lincoln

YOU HAVE SPECIAL TALENTS AND abilities that you can maximize to earn far more than you are earning today. Your goal is to identify those things that you can do in an excellent fashion and then commit yourself wholeheartedly to becoming the best in that part of your chosen field.

One of the qualities of superior men and women is that they are extremely self-reliant. They accept complete responsibility for themselves and everything that happens to them. They look to themselves as the source of their successes and as the main cause of their problems and difficulties. High achievers say, "If it's to be, it's up to me."

When they are not satisfied with something in their work, they ask themselves, "What is it *in me* that is causing this problem?" They refuse to make excuses or blame other people. Instead, they look for ways to overcome obstacles and make progress.

Because they have this attitude of self-employment, they take a strategic approach to their work and careers.

Think Long-Term about Your Career

The essential element in strategic planning for a corporation or a business entity is the concept of *return on equity*. All business planning is aimed at organizing and reorganizing the resources of the business in such a way as to increase the financial returns to the business owners. The focus is on increasing the quantity of output relative to the quantity of input, concentrating on areas of high profitability and return while simultaneously withdrawing resources from areas of low profitability and return.

Companies that plan and act strategically in a rapidly changing environment are the ones that survive and prosper. Companies that fail to engage in this form of strategic thinking are those that fall behind and often disappear.

Increase Your Return on Energy

To achieve everything you are capable of achieving, you also must become a skilled strategic planner in your life and work. But instead of aiming to increase your return on equity, your goal is to increase your *return on energy*.

Most people in America start off in life with little more than their ability to work and generate income. According to Thomas J. Stanley, author of *The Millionaire Next Door*, more than 80 percent of millionaires in America are self-made. They started with nothing at all. Most of them have been broke, or nearly broke, several times during their lifetimes.

Your Personal Services

Most fortunes begin with the sale of personal services. But the people who eventually get to the top are those who think and act in specific ways that set them apart from the average.

Perhaps the most important approach top people take, consciously or unconsciously, is to look at themselves *strategically*. They think about themselves as a bundle of resources, capable of doing many different jobs. They carefully consider how they can best utilize their special combination of knowledge and skills in the marketplace and how they can best capitalize on their strengths and abilities to increase their returns to themselves and their families.

There are four keys to strategically marketing yourself and your services. These are applicable to huge companies such as General Motors, to candidates running for election, and to individuals who want to earn the very most money in their careers.

Think Strategically about Your Career

The first of these four keys is *specialization*. This is essential today. No one can be all things to all people. A *jack-of-all-trades* is usually a master of none. That career path usually leads to a dead end. Specialization is the key. Men and women who are successful have a series of general skills, but they also have one or two *core skills*, which they have developed to a high level so that they can perform in an outstanding manner and do excellent work.

Your decision about how, where, when, and why you are going to specialize in a particular part of your job or career is perhaps the most important decision you will ever make in your career. Strategic planner Michael J. Kami said it well: "Those who do not think about the future cannot have one."

Look into yourself

In determining your area of specialization, put your current job aside for the moment, and take the time to analyze yourself from every point of view. Look at your entire lifetime of activities and accomplishments.

What is *your* area of specialization? What are you especially good at right now? If things continue as they are, on your current growth track, what are you likely to be good at in the future—say one, two, or even five years from now? Is this a marketable skill with a growing demand? Or is your field changing in such a way that you are going to have to change as well if you want to keep up with it?

Looking into the future, in what specific skill areas should you specialize if you want to rise to the top of your field, make an excellent living, and take complete control of your financial future?

How Are You Different and Better?

The second key to marketing yourself strategically is *differentiation*. You must decide what you're going to do to be not only different but also *better* than your competitors in the field you choose. Remember, you only have to be good in *one* specific area to move ahead of the pack. And you must decide what that area should be.

Your area of differentiation is the work you do in an excellent fashion. You do it better than 90 percent of the people in your field. What is your area of excellence today? What *could* it be if you decided to become excellent at a new skill? What *should* it be if you want to get to the top of your field and be one of the highest-paid people in your industry?

What is the most important and valued skill in your business, the one that most contributes to financial results? The greater the impact you can have on sales and profitability, the more valuable you become, and the more money you will earn.

Segment Your Market

The third strategic principle in capitalizing on your strengths is *segmentation*. This requires that you look at the marketplace and determine where you can best apply yourself, with your unique talents and abilities, to earn the highest possible return on energy expended. What customers, companies, and markets can best utilize your special talents and offer you the most in terms of financial rewards and opportunities?

One employer or industry might place a low value on your special talents and abilities, while another type of business might value your skill so highly that they will pay you a lot of money for the results you can get for them.

Concentrate Your Efforts

The final key to personal strategic marketing is *concentration*. Once you have decided on your area of specialization, your means of differentiation, and your market segment, your final job is to concentrate all of your energies on becoming excellent in your specific area and doing an exceptional job. The marketplace pays extraordinary rewards only for extraordinary performance.

In the final analysis, everything that you have done up to now is simply the groundwork for becoming outstanding in your chosen field. When you become very good at doing what people want and need, you begin moving rapidly into the top ranks of the highest-paid people in our society.

{ Your goal is to identify what you are excellent at. Commit wholeheartedly to becoming the best in your chosen field. }

CHAPTER FOUR

EARN WHAT YOU'RE WORTH

"Opportunity often comes disguised in the form of misfortune, or temporary defeat."

–Napoleon Hill

To earn what you are really worth, you have to be in the right job in the first place. Sometimes you could earn more just by walking across the street and getting a new job, if your special talents and skills could be used to get more valuable results for a different employer.

This is a challenging time in human history to be out in the job market, working to survive and thrive. However, in spite of problems in the economy, there are countless opportunities and possibilities for talented people to find or create great jobs and earn more than they ever have before. In spite of the aftermath from the Great Recession, unemployment is relatively low, and people are making money and moving ahead with their lives.

The rate of new business formation is on the rise, and the Bureau of Labor Statistics reports that the number of job openings has risen by more than 5 percent. In 2016, there are more than three million job openings every month. A large number of employers are looking for talented, committed people to help their businesses grow.

The biggest single limit on business success today is the ability to attract and keep good people, like you. More people than ever before are becoming financially successful today as a result of doing an excellent job and being paid well for it. Your job is to participate fully in the new economy, to realize your true income potential by getting and keeping an excellent job, and then moving upward and onward in your career for the rest of your working life.

Develop Your Options

You are only as free as your *options*. The more skilled you become at getting the job you want, the more money you will make and the more choices you will have. Most people start their job search by answering Internet ads, sending out résumés, or using a staffing agency. But the fact is that 85 percent of all jobs available in your community, right now, are not advertised. They do not appear in any media. They are hidden and waiting for you to discover them, like buried treasure.

A self-directed job search enables you to take control of your career and your life. It makes you the architect of your own destiny, giving you a sense of control and a positive attitude. It ensures that you will never be unemployed.

See Yourself as Self-Employed

The starting point of taking control of your career is to begin to view yourself as *self-employed*. See yourself as 100 percent responsible for your life and for everything that happens to you.

As I wrote earlier, you are the president of your own personal service corporation. Every day, every week, and every month, you go into the marketplace and sell the services of your own corporation to the highest bidder.

As president of your own personal service corporation, you are completely responsible for marketing and selling yourself in the marketplace. You are responsible for production—for producing the highest quality and quantity of services of which you are capable. You are responsible for quality control—for doing excellent work at whatever is entrusted to you. You are responsible for research and development—for continually upgrading your knowledge and skills so that you can do your job better and faster. You are responsible for finance—for organizing your financial life in such a way that you accomplish your financial goals. *You* are the president of your own company.

This attitude is the starting point of getting the job you want, not only in the short term, but for the rest of your career.

Decide Exactly What You Want

Most people go into the workplace and take whatever is offered to them. They allow the employer to determine the direction of their careers. That's because many people have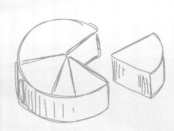

never really given much thought to their careers. Since their first job, they have merely reacted and responded to the demands placed upon them by others as the years went by. But that is not for you.

Here is a series of exercises that you can practice throughout your career to make sure that you are on the right track:

First, describe your *ideal job*. Imagine that you could have any job in the world. Exactly what would that job be? Remember, you can't hit a target you can't see.

Second, look around you in the marketplace. If you could have any job, what *exactly* would it be? If you see a job that you like, go and talk to someone who is doing that job, and ask for their advice. You'll be amazed at the insights that people will offer you in just a few minutes of conversation.

Third, project yourself into the *future*. What sort of work would you like to be doing in three to five years? Everyone has to start at the beginning with a new job or career, but you must be clear about where you want to be in your career in the future. This enables you to make much better decisions when taking a particular job in the first place.

Fourth, consider if you could work anywhere in the country, taking into consideration weather and geography, *where* exactly you would like to work? It is amazing how many people pack up and move to a different part of the country—*before* taking a new job—simply because that is where they have always wanted to live. Could this be true for you?

Fifth, ask yourself what *size* and *type* of company you would like to work for? Would you like to work for a small, medium-sized, or large company? Would you like to work for a high-tech or a low-tech company? Would you like to work for a service or a manufacturing company? Describe your ideal company in as much detail as you possibly can.

Sixth, think about what kind of *people* you would like to work with. Describe your ideal boss. Describe your ideal colleagues. Remember, the quality of the people and your social relationships at work are going to have more impact on your happiness and success than any other factor. Choose your boss and your colleagues with care.

Seventh, determine how much you would like to *earn* in one year. In two years. In five years. This is very important. You should be asking questions about your earning ability and the earnings ceiling at the job interview. Be sure that the job is in a company or situation that enables you to achieve your earnings goals within the time horizon you've projected.

Eighth, ask *who else* is working at the kind of job that you would like to have, or earning the kind of money that you would like to earn. What are they doing differently from you? What qualifications do they have that you still need to acquire?

Ninth, whom do you know who can *help you* position yourself for the kind of job you want? Who can give you advice? Who can point you in the right direction? Whom should you ask for help? Remember, everyone who succeeds does so with the help of other people.

Tenth, what *level of responsibility* do you desire? How high do you want to rise in your career? What title or position would you be most comfortable with?

Clarity Is Essential

The most amazing discovery is this: the more specific and clear you are about exactly what you want to do, where you want to do it, and how much you want to earn, the easier it is for someone to hire you and pay you the kind of money you want to make. Go back over these questions and answer them one by one before you start looking for the job you want.

Your job is to participate fully
in the new economy, to realize
your true income potential by
getting and keeping an excellent
job, and then moving upward
and onward in your career for
the rest of your working life.

CHAPTER FIVE

GET GOOD AT WHAT YOU DO

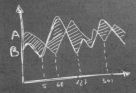

"The big secret of life is that there is no secret. Whatever your goal, you can get there if you're willing to work."

—OPRAH WINFREY

WE ARE LIVING IN THE most advanced age of humankind. It has never been possible to live better or longer than people live right now, and if anything, it will only get better in the years ahead.

You are extraordinary. There never has been and never will be anyone in the world with the same unique combination of talents, abilities, knowledge, experience, insights, desires, goals, and ambitions that you have. The odds of there being another person who is just like you are more than 50 billion to one, which is another way of saying that it will never happen.

At birth, a baby's brain contains 100 billion neurons. Each cell in your brain is connected to as many as 20,000 other cells by dendrites and ganglia. The popular psychologist Tony Buzan has estimated that 100 billion neurons taken to the 20,000th power means that the number of thoughts your brain can create is greater than the number of all the molecules in the known universe. The amount would be equivalent to the number one followed by ten pages of zeros. In a single day alone, you think about 70,000 thoughts with little effort or concentration.

The Smarter You Get, the Smarter You Get

The wonderful thing about your incredible mind is that it is like a muscle. The more you use it, the stronger and more flexible it becomes. Unfortunately, the opposite is also true. If you don't use it, you lose it. Without constant exercising and stretching, your brain becomes weaker and soon loses much of its alertness and speed.

The fact is that, whatever you are earning, you should be earning twice as much as you are right now. The only question you should be asking is, "Why aren't I *already* earning that amount?"

When I ask my audiences this question in seminars, they immediately start to think of all the reasons they aren't already earning twice as much. And what I have found over the years is that all those reasons are merely *excuses*. They are limiting beliefs that hold people back. These excuses usually have no substance, no foundation in reality. They are merely ideas for earning less than the excuse-maker is truly worth, ideas that he or she has accepted, usually unthinkingly, and learned to live with.

Starting from Behind

When I started off my adult life, I had few advantages. I had dropped out of high school and worked at laboring jobs for several years before I got into sales. In sales, I spun my wheels for many months, barely earning enough to survive and pay for my room in a small boardinghouse.

Then one day, I began asking, "Why is it that some people are more successful than others?"

I noticed that there were people all around me, including people younger than I was, who also had limited educations and had come from poor backgrounds, who seemed to be doing better than I was. They were earning more money, driving better cars (whereas I had no car at all), and wearing nicer clothes. In the evenings, they went to nice restaurants and nightclubs, and on the weekends, they went to beautiful resorts and took expensive vacations. This mystified me. Why were some people doing so well, while the rest of us were struggling?

The Great Question

Then I did something that changed my life. I went to the most successful man in my company, a sales guy who was earning ten times as much as anyone else, and I asked him why he was more successful than I was. What was he doing differently than I and all the other salespeople were doing?

He quite willingly offered to help. He first asked me to explain to him how I was selling, how I was approaching prospects, and what I was saying to them. I couldn't answer. I was approaching every customer differently, saying whatever fell out of my mouth.

He then told me that I was doing it all *wrong*. He described how to open a sales conversation, develop rapport with the prospect, ask good questions, and talk about my product intelligently. He explained that selling, like any other field, is made up of a definite series of steps—a process—and that if you follow them, you will make more sales than if you don't.

Do What Top People Do

So I did what he told me to. I began asking more questions and focused on building rapport and trust with prospects. I took the time to learn about their situations and needs relative to what I was selling. I began to match my products with their specified needs, answered their questions or concerns, and *asked* them to buy my product. And they did. And my sales and my income went up and up.

Within a year, my income had doubled and then tripled. Soon I was teaching the same professional selling process that I had learned from people who had never sold anything before. And their incomes went up and up as well. Today, many years later, many of those salespeople are millionaires and multimillionaires, owning and operating multiple businesses.

The Iron Law of the Universe

What I learned was the law of *cause and effect*. This law says that for every *effect*, there is a *cause.* If you can identify the effect that you desire, you can trace it back to a cause or causes. If you then duplicate the causes, you will soon get the effect you want.

In other words, if you do what other successful, highly paid people do, you will soon get the same results they do and become a successful, highly paid person yourself. There is no mystery.

The great challenge is that the world is full of people who are doing what *failures* do and are amazed when they get the same results that failures get. They are implementing the same causes and getting the same effects. This is happening *by law*, not by chance.

Nature is neutral. Nature doesn't *care*. Whatever you sow, you eventually reap. Whatever you put in, you get out. If you fail to put it in, you fail to get it out. The best part of the law of cause and effect is that, whatever goal you can set for yourself, or whatever success you desire, if you simply do what other people have done before to achieve the same result, you can, within reason, have it as well.

Change Your Mind-Set

What is the difference between people in the bottom 80 percent and people in the top 20 percent? Simple.
People in the top 20 percent have a different mind-set from people in the bottom 80 percent. Not only do the words they use have different meanings, but their thinking styles are different as well.

Top people are in *continual learning mode*.

They are curious, interested, and eager to absorb new knowledge. They are hungry to learn. They read, listen to audio programs, attend seminars, and ask questions of people who know more than they do. They are great listeners. They take notes during every seminar and conversation.

Income and Information Go Together

The people in the top 20 percent see that there is a direct link between new information and increased income. They never stop improving. They know that one of the best time-management tools in the world is to get *better* at what you do. Geoffrey Colvin, author of the bestselling book *Talent Is Overrated*, refers to this as "deliberate practice."

The people who get ahead faster than others are those who deliberately invest the time and put in the hard work to learn and practice new, essential skills that can help them advance up the ladder of their careers. They never stop learning and growing. Their entire focus is to push to the front.

The Only Real Difference

In its simplest terms, the difference between people at the bottom of the ladder and people at the top is practical knowledge and skill. The people who are ahead today, and getting further ahead, are those who have the knowledge and skill that they require to excel in their fields. They continually add to that knowledge and skill.

Just as money grows with compound interest, knowledge and skills also grow through compounding. Each bit of valuable information that you learn makes your mind like Velcro, enabling you to recognize and hook onto other pieces of information that can help you do your job even better than before.

It's sort of a mental thinking & curiosity. of looking at the curious & creative way.

attitude about critical

It's about mind-set

world in a playful &

—Adam Savage

CHAPTER SIX

RESULTS ARE EVERYTHING

"In the end, it is important to remember that we cannot become what we need to be by remaining what we are."

–Max DePree

WHAT YOU ARE ABOUT TO learn in this chapter can change your life. These ideas, methods, and techniques can increase your efficiency and effectiveness, boost your productivity, double your income, lower your stress levels, and make you one of the most productive and valuable people in your business or field today. They are the *indispensable* keys to earning what you are really worth.

All successful, highly paid people are very *productive*. They work longer hours and put more into each hour. They get a lot more done than the average person, get paid more, and get promoted faster. They become leaders and role models and are highly respected and esteemed by everyone around them. Inevitably, they rise to the top of their fields and to the top of their income ranges, and so can you.

Every single one of these tested and proven strategies for managing your time and doubling your productivity is learnable through practice and repetition. Each of these methods, if you practice it regularly, will eventually become a habit of both thinking and working.

When you begin applying these techniques to your work and to your life, your self-esteem, self-confidence, self-respect, and sense of personal pride will go up immediately. The payoff for you will be tremendous and will last the rest of your life.

Make a Decision!

Every positive change in your life begins with a clear, unequivocal decision that you are going to either do something or stop doing something. Significant change only begins for you when you decide to either get in or get out—either *fish or cut bait*.

Decisiveness is one of the most important qualities of successful and happy men and women, and decisiveness is developed through practice and repetition, over and over again, until it becomes as natural to you as breathing in and breathing out.

The sad fact is that most people are poor because they have not yet *decided* to be rich. Most people are overweight and unfit because they have not yet *decided* to be thin and fit. Most people are inefficient time wasters because they haven't yet *decided* to be highly productive in everything they do.

Decide today that you are going to become an expert in time management and personal productivity, no matter how long it takes or how much you invest to achieve it. Resolve today that you are going to practice these principles over and over again until they become second nature.

Practice Self-Discipline in Everything

Discipline yourself to do what you know you need to do to be the very best in your field. Perhaps the best definition of self-discipline comes from writer Elbert Hubbard: "Self-discipline is the ability to make yourself do what you should do, when you should do it, whether you feel like it or not."

It is easy to do something when you feel like it. It's when you don't feel like it, but you force yourself to do it anyway, that you move your life and career onto the fast track.

What decisions do you need to make today in order to start moving toward the top of your field? Whatever the decision is, to get in or to get out, make it today and then get started. This single act can change the whole direction of your life.

Develop Clear Goals and Objectives

Perhaps the most important word in achieving success for the rest of your life is the word *clarity*. Fully 80 percent of your success comes about as the result of your being absolutely clear about what it is you are trying to accomplish. Unfortunately, probably 80 percent

or more of failure and frustration comes to people who are vague or fuzzy about what it is they want and how to go about achieving it.

The great oil billionaire H. L. Hunt once said that there are only *two* real requirements for great success. First, he said, "Decide what you want, decide what you are willing to exchange for it." Most people never do this. Second, he said, "Establish your priorities and go to work."

You can have just about anything you really want as long as you are willing to pay the price. And nature always demands two things: that you pay the price *in full* and that you pay it *in advance.*

Plan Every Day in Advance

Daily planning is absolutely essential for doubling your productivity and your income. You should practice the *Six P Formula* for high achievement. This formula spells out the message "Proper Prior Planning Prevents Poor Performance."

Proper planning is the mark of the professional. Successful

men and women take a good deal of time to plan their activities in advance. Spending 10 percent of your time on planning your activities before you begin will save you as much as 90 percent of the time necessary to perform those activities once you start work.

Begin with a List

Begin by making a *master list* of everything you can think of that you have to do in the long term. This master list then becomes the central control list for your life. Whenever you think of something new that you have to do, or want to do, write it down on your master list.

At the beginning of each month, make a *monthly list* covering everything that you can think of that you will have to do in the coming weeks. Then, break your monthly list down into a *weekly list*, and specify exactly when you are going to start and complete the tasks that you have decided upon for your month. Finally, and perhaps most importantly, make a *daily list* of your activities, preferably the night before, so that your unconscious mind can work on your list while you sleep.

Always work from a list. When something new comes up during the day, write it down on your list before you do it. As you work, tick off each item as you complete it. This gives you an ongoing sense of accomplishment and a feeling of personal progress. Crossing off items one by one motivates you and actually gives you more energy. A list serves as a scorecard and makes you feel like a winner. It tells you where you are making progress and what you have to do the next day.

According to time-management experts, working from a list will increase your productivity by 25 percent from the very first day. Almost all highly effective people think on paper and work from written lists.

Use the *ABCDE* Method to Set Priorities

This is one of the most powerful time-management techniques for setting priorities that you will ever learn. And the beauty of this method lies in the fact that it is so simple and easy to use.

The key to doubling your productivity, in any area of your work or at any time of your life, is to select your *most valuable task* and then discipline yourself to work on that task until it is complete. All of time management revolves around helping you clarify, in your own mind, before you start, the most important thing you could possibly be doing.

The way that you determine your highest priority at any moment is to think about the potential *consequences* of doing or not doing a particular task. An important task is one that can have major consequences if it is done or not done. All highly productive people think continually about possible consequences as they plan and organize their activities.

Important and unimportant

With the *ABCDE* Method, you make a list of everything that you have to do *before* you begin work. You then go through the list carefully and put one of these letters next to each item on the list.

An *A* item is something that is important and urgent. This is something that you *must* do, something that has *serious* consequences associated with either doing it or not doing it. Put an *A* next to every key task on your list.

A *B* item is something that you *should* do, but it is not as important as an *A* task. There are consequences associated with doing it or not doing it, but they are only mild consequences that don't last long.

A *C* item is something that would be *nice* to do, but for which there are no consequences at all. Phoning a friend, going for coffee, reading the newspaper, or chatting with a coworker are all things that are nice to do, but they have absolutely no consequences for your career or your success.

Follow the rules

The rule is that you should never do a *B* item when there is an *A* item left undone. You should never do a *C* item when there is a *B* item left undone. You must be very disciplined about this. *ABC* items are priorities.

A *D* item is an item that you *delegate* or outsource to someone else who can do it as well or almost as well as you. The rule is that you should delegate everything possible to free up more time for you to concentrate on your *A* activities.

E is an item that you can *eliminate*. These are items that are of such low priority that you could eliminate them completely and it would make no difference at all. Sometimes, the disciplined act of eliminating low-value tasks can simplify your life and free up enough time for you to accomplish those tasks that have the greatest possible consequences for you.

Once you have applied the *ABCDE* Method to your list, go back over the list and organize your *A* tasks by priority. Put an

A-1 next to your most important task, an *A-2* next to your second most important task, and so on.

Then, begin immediately on your *A-1* task and discipline yourself to stay at it until it is finished. This simple *ABCDE* Method alone will double your productivity.

Make Every Minute Count

We are living in one of the most challenging times in all of human history. But there are few limits to what you can accomplish, beyond the limits that you place on yourself. Your job is to become one of the most productive people in your field. Your goal is to develop a reputation for being the person others come to *first* when anyone wants or needs something done.

Your goal is to get paid more, to get promoted faster, and to have a wonderful life. You can achieve it by managing your time and doubling your productivity.

The important

to have a great

determination to

thing in life is

aim and the

attain it. -GOETHE

CHAPTER SEVEN

SUPERCHARGE YOUR CAREER

"We must all suffer from one of two pains: the pain of discipline or the pain of regret. The difference is that discipline weighs ounces while regret weighs tons."

–Jim Rohn

Have you noticed that some people receive more promotions and greater pay than their colleagues, even though they don't seem to be more competent or capable than others? This doesn't seem fair. Why should some people get ahead while others, who seem to be working just as hard, and sometimes even harder, get passed over for promotion and the additional rewards that go with it?

The fact is that to be a great success, it is important not only to be good at what you do, but also to be *perceived* as being good at what you do. Human beings are creatures of perception. It is not what they see but what they think they see that determines how they think and act.

If your coworker is perceived as being more promotable than you are, for whatever reasons, then it is very likely that your coworker will get additional responsibilities and more money, even though you know that you could do a better job if given the chance.

Supercharging Your Career

Fortunately, however, there are several things that you can do to increase your visibility and accelerate the speed at which you move ahead in your career.

The starting point of attaining higher visibility is for you to develop a high level of competence to become very good at the most important things you do. Determine what parts of your job are most important to your boss and to your company, and then make the decision to become excellent in those areas.

To stand out, you must be perceived as being very good at what you do. Your future depends on it. This perception alone will bring you to the attention of key people faster than you can imagine. The perception of excellent performance will open up opportunities for greater responsibilities, higher pay, and better positions. Becoming good at what you do should be the foundation of your strategy for gaining higher visibility and rapid advancement in your career.

Employers everywhere are looking for men and women of *action*, people who will get in there and get the job done right, as soon as possible. When you develop a reputation for competence and the predictable delivery of results, you quickly become visible to all the key people in your working environment.

Look the Part of Success

Excellence at what you do is essential, but it's not enough. There are additional elements that go into the  perception that others have of you. And one of the most important elements is your overall *image*, from head to toe. How you appear to others makes a real difference.

Human resources executives typically make the decision to hire within the first *thirty seconds* of an interview. Many people believe that the decision to accept or reject a job candidate is actually made in the first *four seconds*. Many capable men and women are disqualified from job opportunities before they open their mouths, because they simply do not *look the part*.

There are many elements of your life over which you have no control and that you cannot choose. But your external dress and appearance are totally a matter of *personal* preference. Through your choice of clothes, your grooming, and your overall appearance, you deliberately make a statement about the kind of person you really are. The way you look on the outside is a representation of the way you see yourself on the inside. If you have a positive, professional self-image, you will take pains to make your external appearance consistent with it.

You should dress the way the senior people in your company dress—birds of a feather flock together. People like to interact with and promote people who look the way they do.

Even better, dress for the position two jobs above your own. Since people judge you largely by the way you look on the outside, be sure to look like a professional. The result will be that the impression you make on people who can help advance your career will be positive. They will open doors for you in ways that you cannot now imagine.

Join Professional Associations

Another powerful way to increase your visibility is to join one or two professional associations connected with your business or field. Begin by attending meetings as a guest, to carefully assess whether or not a professional association can be of value to you. Determine whether the members are the kind of people you would like to know, people who are well established in their careers, or at the top of their businesses. Once you have decided that becoming known to the key people in this association can advance your career, join, and get involved.

Get Involved

Most people who join any club or association do little more than attend the regular meetings. For some reason, they feel that they are too busy to assist with the various jobs that need to get done. But this is not for you. Your goal is to pick a key committee and volunteer to serve on it.

Find out which committee seems to be the most active and influential in the organization, and then step up to the plate. Volunteer your time, expertise, and energy, and get busy. Attend every meeting. Take careful notes. Ask for assignments, and complete them on time and in an excellent fashion.

By getting involved, you create an opportunity to *perform* for key people in your profession in a nonthreatening environment. You give them a chance to see what you can do and what kind of a person you are. You expand your range of valuable contacts in one of the most effective ways possible in our country today. The people you get to know on these committees can eventually be extremely helpful to you in your work and in your career.

Upgrade Your Skills

Another way to increase your visibility is to continually upgrade your work-related skills, and to make sure that your superiors know about it. Look for additional courses you can take to improve at your job, and discuss them with your boss. Ask him or her to pay for the courses, if he or she will, but make it clear that you're going to take them anyway.

A young woman who worked for me was able to double her salary in less than six months by aggressively learning the computer, bookkeeping, and accounting skills she needed as our company grew. And she was worth every penny. We were happy to pay her twice as much.

Ask your boss for book, seminar, and audio-program recommendations. Then follow up by reading and listening to them and asking for further recommendations. Bosses are very impressed with people who are constantly striving to learn more to increase their value to their companies. Doing this regularly can really accelerate your career.

Your Most Valuable Asset

In the final analysis, *you* are your most valuable asset. In financial terms, your ability to earn money—your earning power—is the most important monetary part of your life.

Fortunately, your earning power is not fixed. You start off at your first job with little or no earning power, and from then on, you are in charge for the rest of your life.

When you work to make yourself more valuable, to get more and better results, there is no limit to how much you can earn.

Good luck!

I've learned that fear limits you and your vision. It serves as blinders to what may be just a few steps down the road for you. The journey is valuable, but believing in your talents, your abilities, and your self-worth can empower you to walk down an even brighter path. Transforming fear into freedom - how great is that? —Soledad O'Brian

ABOUT THE
AUTHOR

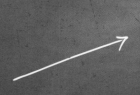

Brian Tracy is the chairman of Brian Tracy International, a human resources development company headquartered in Solana Beach, California. He has written seventy books and produced more than eight hundred audio and video training programs. His materials have been translated into forty-two languages and are used in sixty-four countries. He is active in community affairs and serves as a consultant to several nonprofit organizations.

Brian is also one of the top professional speakers and trainers in the world today. He addresses more than 250,000 men and women each year on the subjects of leadership, strategy, sales, and personal and business success. He has given more than five thousand talks and seminars to five million people worldwide, bringing a unique blend of humor, insight, information, and inspiration.

Brian lives with his wife, Barbara, and their four children in Solana Beach, California, and is an avid student of business, psychology, management, sales, history, economics, politics, metaphysics, and religion. He believes that each person has extraordinary untapped potential that he or she can learn to access and, in doing so, can accomplish more in a few years than the average person does in a lifetime.

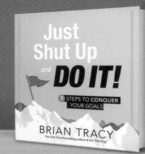
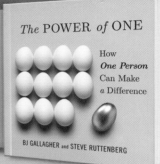